I Think I Must Have Swallowed The Sun

Lauren Kelly

India | USA | UK

Made with ❤ on the BookLeaf Publishing Platform
www.bookleafpub.in
www.bookleafpub.com

Dedication

For Christian,

for pushing me when i need it,
and inspiring me to live again.

Preface

This book of poems is generally speaking, a mess. It's intended to be that way, as the experiences I write about are messy. C'est la vie.

As with all things, take what resonates, and leave what doesn't.

Acknowledgements

First off, thank you to BookLeaf publishing for this amazing opportunity. I've had so much fun writing these past few weeks, and I'm excited to share what I've come up with. I want to give a huge thank you to my partner for supporting me throughout this process and pushing me to meet my potential. Thank you also to my best friend for having to watch all of the heartbreak I write about in this book firsthand, and somehow still putting up with me.

And thank you to anyone reading this, for caring about what I have to say.

the flame

i asked the flame about you,
and she wavered with distaste and disapproval.
i blamed it on my credulity,
pulling you closer despite her warning.

but you?

you burned us to the fucking ground.

to be known

the desire to be seen runs deep
the desire to be known runs deeper
and the desire to be understood runs deepest of all

~ you didn't even know my middle name

crush (me)

sometimes i wrap my intimacy with platonic paper
and neatly tied bows of friendly adoration

wolf in sheep's clothing

you are a wolf in sheep's clothing
but we can all see your matted fur beneath the wool,
your lethal fangs and claws on display
but you still think you have me fooled?

helplessness

i am 5, and i am wide-eyed, overwhelmed.
the sting of a scolding burns hot across my cheeks. tears
brimming in my eyes with childish shame, lip quivering
with the helplessness of youth.

i am 18, and the yelling.
oh god the yelling.
the pressure to respond correctly holds me delicately,
like a marionette on your strings. but we both know
there is no appeasing you. i'm just an outlet for your
mental illness. i've sewn my mouth shut to prevent my
words from bleeding into your anger. instead i sit silent
and stoic amidst your bellowing -
"say something. SAY SOMETHING. SAY SOMETHI-"

i am 21, and the rage within you is spilling into me.
i feel your violence burn through my veins and tear at
my stitches until my fury pours out. the newfound
respect i see in your eyes is so rewarding that this
becomes our new vicious pattern, and we call it love.

i am 23, and with you i am finally safe.
but anger still smolders inside of me from the fire that
others built before you. i watch as my words cut into you

and i see how sharp my tongue has become. your divine
blood drips onto the floor, and i feel that childish
helplessness rise in my throat once more to re-introduce
herself as regret.

blackout

liquor tugs at my consciousness
as your impure fingers defile my sacred flesh
tearing my innocence and staining my spirit
with the blood of who I once was

burn

save me from the frigid sting of loneliness and burn me
with what you call love

i thought about visiting your mother's grave

i wouldn't know where to find it,
but i could walk the lawn until i did.
i would tell her about you.
i'd tell her i liked your smile,
and i'd tell her you're kind to me.
i'd tell her about the dates you took me on,
and i'd tell her that you paid.
i'd tell her about that concert we went to last week,
and i'd tell her how you carry the weight of positivity on
your back.
i'd tell her you took care of me while i was sick,
and i'd tell her we talked about kids.
i'd tell her that i thought you'd make a good dad,
and i'd tell her she would be proud of who you have
become.

i'd tell her that i knew we weren't built to last,
but most of all,
 i'd tell her how i loved you anyway.

predictability

i'm just another wounded soul with pretty words
running through my veins

my addiction is...

my addiction is a lover.
and she is much softer than i expected her to be, with the sweet caress of her mirage, and her gift of rose colored glasses she is so alluring, with her wholly captivating glow.

my addiction is a child.
and she is spoiled. she is needy. she is persistent. she needs more, more, MORE. she is insatiable and temperamental, and if i don't give her what she wants she'll scream, but it will be my voice ringing in your ears.

my addiction is a ghost.
and she haunts me, playing tricks on my mind. she offers empty promises of relief in exchange for possession of my body and ownership of my soul. i want to refuse, but god is she persuasive.

my addiction is a stalker.
and she is entitled. she finds me, chases me, follows me home. she welcomes herself in where she was not invited, taking whatever she can get her determined hands on, and displaying it like trophies of conquest.

my addiction is a murderer.
and before i can run, she reveals a knife in hand. she
preys on the people i love, severs our ties, and turns back
to me. blood spills down my back, and i feel my old self
fade from my eyes.

pedestal

find me on my knees at your feet,
look upon me and forgive me for my sins.
allow me to cross the threshold of your Eden
and I will devote myself to you

betrayal

it creates a different kind of wound
when the person that abandons you
is yourself

the worst part

is that after all of that
i stayed

and i still wasn't enough for you

there's a girl in the mirror

there's a girl in the mirror
and she's wearing my face
but her eyes look a bit different
they've sunken into place

her features look sharper
i wonder if she eats?
and her poor broken heart inside
i see it weakly beats

her skin is pale but touched
with marks of black and blue
and though she tries to cover them
i still can count a few

she has lost any hope
from friends she has withdrawn
without a clue of where to turn
it's hard to carry on

i'm the girl in the mirror
though i'm not her anymore
you pushed and pushed until i left
and now i've closed that door

to the girl in the mirror
i'm sorry it went that far
i hope my past can see me now
and is proud of who we are

breathing

the morning is young
and i lie awake
feeling the rise and fall of your chest
listening to the steady rhythm of your breath

we rouse in the sunlight
and our eyes meet
captivating me completely
stealing the breath from my lungs

the day passes and we meet again
each carrying the chaos of our days
but we hold tightly to one another
slowing our breath and returning home

night falls upon us
and we lie together once more
pressing tight to each other
intertwined souls accompanied by panting breath

oh how deeply i must love you
for something as regular as breathing
to feel so divine

radiance

i beam so brightly next to you
i think i must have swallowed the sun

naïveté

i would like to believe i've healed, but i still feel the ache of shame in my chest when i remember the betrayal of how i used to let you love me.

persephone woman

i am a persephone woman
and you my delusional spring,
but i shudder in your frigid breeze
i shiver with the sting

your blinding sun retreats behind
what i wished wasn't true
clarity reveals my own personal hell
here, in this bed *with you*

skin

there is a monster plaguing my reflection.

she looks at my bare figure, examining my scars and her
face twists with dissatisfaction.
she tugs at my flesh, pinpointing imperfections, dragging
her nails across me and leaving red lines in her wake.
she digs her claws into me, muttering about perfection,
ripping out flaw after flaw and filling my nose with the
scent of iron.
she tears into my chest, and carves through layers of
skin and bone.
she hungers for satisfaction and she is driven entirely
mad with bloodlust.

my heart is exposed.

my lungs are heaving.

and as i turn to confront the monster in the mirror,
i find i'm the only figure in the reflection
and i swear i catch a glimpse of madness leaving my own
eyes.

singed sleeves and heart thieves

it was you that placed this rage inside my chest
and you who fed the flame until it swallowed me whole
and yet the slightest singe of your sleeve
was enough for you to walk away

there is a stillness within me

there is a stillness within me
and she has taken my restlessness by the hands,
and said, with a gentle voice and a soft smile,
 "you've done enough, i'll take it from here"

with his trembling hands and aching limbs,
my restlessness surrenders.
he relinquishes my rage,
and intrusts her with my insecurity,
sheds my shame,
and turns over my troubles,
lay down my loneliness,
and abandons my anguish,
gives up my grief,
and hands over my hatred.

my stillness bears it all,
and finally my restlessness lets me go

~ this must be what healing feels like